how can we encourage a fresh expression?

Share booklet 09

This *Share booklet* is one of a series which aims to help you to think about how to start, support and sustain a fresh expression of church.

01 how can fresh expressions emerge?

02 how should we start?

03 what should we start?

04 how can we get support?

05 how can we find our way?

06 how can we be sustainable?

07 how can we be a great team?

08 how can we finance a fresh expression?

09 how can we encourage a fresh expression?

10 how should we teach and preach?

Share booklets 01-08 are available as a combined volume, *Starting and sustaining a fresh expression of church.*

Contents

Take a first step

How can we encourage a fresh expression? explores how to encourage and support a fresh expression through your local church.

Signs of life

The vision for a fresh expression of church emerges in all sorts of ways, often through a sense of godly disquiet. The initiative will be shaped by who leads it, whom it serves, the particularities of the context and by the Holy Spirit. And fresh expressions of church are increasingly on the radar of the local church.

Maybe:

- a member of your congregation wants to start a fresh expression of church;
- as a minister, you have been asked to oversee the training of an ordained pioneer;
- your church wants to encourage a fresh expression as part of its mission;
- your church has launched missional communities to serve people outside the church;
- you have a pastoral ministry and don't see how that can fit into the fresh expressions vision;
- you belong to a group of local churches that is starting a fresh expression.

How might you offer proper support?

The first thing to bear in mind is that each fresh expression is unique, so support must be tailored to its specific needs. What follows are some of the issues to keep in mind. But remember, there is no blueprint - support will look different in different settings. Prayer is fundamental at every point.

Understand fresh expressions

It may seem obvious to start by understanding fresh expressions of church. Yet it is extraordinary how many people think they understand fresh expressions without properly exploring what is involved.

Four characteristics

Fresh expressions have four characteristics. They are:

- **missional** - they work mainly with people outside the church;
- **contextual** - they fit the circumstances of the people they serve;
- **formational** - they aim to make disciples;
- **ecclesial** - they are, or seek to become, church in their own right, they are not stepping stones to an existing congregation.

Fresh expressions are firmly rooted in Scripture and the Christian tradition:

- they are the latest instalment in the 2000-year history of starting new Christian communities as vital to the church's mission;
- they adapt to, but also challenge the surrounding culture, as did Jesus in the incarnation;
- they echo Paul's approach to founding churches in the New Testament;
- they respond to the missional situation we face in 'the West' by serving people whom the church does not now reach;
- they are part of a 'mixed economy', in which new and existing forms of church play different missional roles alongside each other in mutual support.

 Stories and examples of fresh expressions of church
freshexpressions.org.uk/stories

The Guide
freshexpressions.org.uk/guide

 web

 fresh! An introduction to fresh expressions of church and pioneer ministry
David Goodhew, Andrew Roberts, Michael Volland, SCM Press, 2012, 978-033404387-4

Church for every context: An introduction to theology and practice
Michael Moynagh, SCM Press, 2012, 978-033404369-0

mission-shaped church: church planting and fresh expressions of church in a changing context (2nd edition)
Graham Cray, CHP, 2009, 978-071514189-2

 Book

How can fresh expressions emerge? (Share booklet 01)
Michael Moynagh, Andy Freeman, Fresh Expressions,
2011, 978-095681231-5

freshexpressions.org.uk/share/booklets

BOOK

Most fresh expressions, especially if they reach people with little church background, come into being through a prayerful process of:

- listening carefully to God and a specific group of people outside the church, to discern how best to serve them;
- loving and serving these people - with them and for them;
- forming community with and among those being served;
- providing opportunities for individuals to explore becoming disciples of Jesus;
- allowing church to take shape around people who come to faith;
- encouraging the new church to start a further one;
- connecting to other expressions of church.

This process, which varies hugely from one context to another, is described more fully in the Share booklet, *How can fresh expressions emerge?*. It can be portrayed diagrammatically like this:

listening → loving and serving → building community → exploring discipleship → church taking shape → doing it again

What emerges is often unpredictable. The destination is not visible at the start of the journey. So those who oversee fresh expressions must be prepared for surprises and not be over-prescriptive about the outcome. The Spirit may lead the initiative into unexpected territory. At the same time, founders of fresh expressions need some sense of direction and purpose.

Keys to success

To be fruitful, alongside prayer, a fresh expression needs:

- **a faithful and suitably gifted leader supported by a team or small community.**

  The team is vital. But beware of involving too many Christians. Experience shows that a crowd of believers tends to create a Christian sub-culture, which puts off people outside the church.

- **careful contextualisation.**

  This requires constant listening to the people the initiative is called to work with so that it can love and serve them most effectively. It means finding a way to lovingly serve people that is genuinely responsive to them. Don't assume that a successful model elsewhere will necessarily be best for your context - consult the people you seek to serve! If you are inspired by a model, ask how it should be adapted. Adapting a model or doing something new shows that you respect and value the distinctiveness of your context. Contextualisation includes connecting the gospel to individuals' longings, needs, questions and patterns of thought. It involves enabling new believers to become fruitful disciples in their everyday lives. It includes teaching and worship that both relate to the surrounding culture and challenge it. Hospitality and holiness are two sides of the same coin.

- **a clear mission focus.**

  It is much easier to focus the fresh expression on a specific group of people than on individuals from a wide variety of backgrounds, of different ages and with different agendas. As people come to faith, connections need to be made with the wider church so that like-minded people do not exclusively meet together.

- **attention to discipleship and sustainability from the beginning.**

  These are too important to be after-thoughts. They should be at the front of the team's thinking from the earliest stage, even though what they will eventually look like may be far from clear. The team should keep asking, 'What must we do next to lay down paths to discipleship and being sustainable?' This will make discipleship and sustainability intentional goals rather than vague hopes.

You can turn these keys to success into helpful questions when talking with someone starting a fresh expression of church. If the person is thinking of starting a Messy Church for instance, you might ask, 'How would you check out that this is the most appropriate way to serve these families? How might you need to adapt it? Once people come regularly on a monthly basis, can you envisage how they might be taken on a journey to mature faith?'

Lay deep foundations

Five foundations are especially important: prepare the church, select leaders carefully, start with what the founder has got, allow time to gather a team and encourage experimentation.

1. Prepare the church

Being Church, Doing Life
Michael Moynagh, Monarch Books,
2014, 978-085721493-5

First, you must prepare your congregation. Lay and ordained pioneers often battle against the misunderstanding of their fellow Christians. To have the full backing of their local church is a wonderful support. So spend time convincing your leaders and church members of the missional need for fresh expressions of church. Explain how fresh expressions can be a source of hope for the future.

If you are an apparently flourishing church, ask 'Who are we not reaching?' A fresh expression can connect with people outside your orbit.

If the congregation is small and struggling, stress the difference that one or two people can make. Find some small, resonant examples among the stories of fresh expressions of church.

In providing a theological rationale, explain that God does not want mission through the week to be done by individuals alone, but in community wherever possible. The Holy Spirit does mission in Community - with the Father and the Son. Jesus did mission in community with his disciples.

God wants these communities for mission to be in everyday life - Jesus sent his disciples in pairs not to the synagogues, but to the villages and towns (Luke 9.1-6, 10.1). New Testament churches met in people's homes, which were the centre of networks, domesticity and work.

Why not invite your leaders and other church members to read the first two chapters of *Being Church, Doing Life* - besides offering theological reasons for growing fresh expressions of church, the books is full of inspiring stories and practical wisdom.

You might also stress the importance of contextualisation. God speaks through Scripture in different ways according to the context. The incarnation is the supreme example of contextualisation.

All churches contextualise. Your church has adapted to the circumstances of those who attend - otherwise they wouldn't come! Contextualisation is nothing new. Churchgoers agree the time, length, style and format of their meetings, but without reference to the circumstances and needs of those who do not yet attend. As they begin a journey to Jesus, why shouldn't people as yet outside the church determine the nature of their meetings?

Encourage realistic expectations. A fresh expression is not a new way to entice people into church on Sunday. It seeks to become a worshipping community in its own right. You will need to keep saying this since it takes a long time for many people to 'get' it.

Keep reminding people that once you have decided to meet in a certain place, at a certain time, with certain people and with a certain agenda (such as to worship in a particular way), you are bound to include some people and exclude others. Fresh expressions of church are a way of reaching those others. Keep repeating this until it is firmly in people's minds. But don't give the impression that the new gathering will be completely separate. As it comes to maturity, there will be ways for the old and new congregations to enrich each other: one heavy metal congregation met monthly with its Anglo-Catholic neighbour!

Excite your church about the potential partnership. Those who come to faith through a fresh expression of church may bring new gifts, perspectives and - dare one say it - money to the existing congregation. Conversely, longstanding Christians can pass on their experience and understanding of the faith to new believers.

Some people refer to the mixed economy, mixed ecology, blended church or river-and-lake church (rivers flow into a lake and renew it whilst lakes provide an oasis to the life around them). Whatever the language, the theme is the same: existing and new expressions of church serve different people in different ways and bring complementary gifts into the kingdom.

mission shaped congregations: re-imagining church
Colin Brown, Ben Clymo, Norman Ivison,
Fresh Expressions, 2009, 978-095600052-1
freshexpressions.org.uk/resources/congregations

Resources for envisioning a church or congregation

mission shaped congregations: re-imagining church

An interactive DVD-ROM to help you plan a mission-shaped Sunday worship service that introduces fresh expressions, or to aid discussion in small groups, midweek meetings or among your church leaders.

Includes sermon notes, prayers, reflections, hymn and song suggestions, activities, a children's talk and a short video sequence. Materials can be mixed and matched from four different 'streams'. Also included are a PowerPoint presentation and discussion notes for use in midweek meetings, small groups, church councils or PCC meetings.

mission shaped intro

mission shaped intro helps people to reconnect with the communities they are called to serve and to re-imagine the forms of church needed for the 21st century. It features six 90 or 120-minute sessions which include creative activities, film clips, presentations, discussion, worship and prayer. It is ideal for those starting from scratch as well as those who have attended a *vision day* or who are thinking about joining the *mission shaped ministry* course.

vision days

Thousands of Christians all across the UK and worldwide have discovered more about fresh expressions through these fun and interactive days. Using the latest material, now available are twin-track *vision days*, with parallel sessions for enquirers and practitioners and *vision days* especially tailored to new housing estates and the rural context.

mission shaped intro
freshexpressions.org.uk/missionshapedintro

vision days
freshexpressions.org.uk/vision

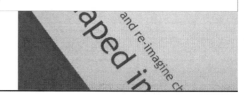

2. Select leaders carefully

There is no foolproof way to prevent things going wrong. Look at all the problems Paul addressed in Corinth! But selecting the right leader will minimise the risks.

Leaders should be:

* **grounded spiritually**

  Having a faithful walk with Jesus, and a commitment to their local church if they are acting in its name.

* **gatherers of people**

  Able to gather a team and to help attract round it the people the initiative serves.

* **gifted in drawing out others**

  Being aware of their limitations, able to involve others with complementary gifts and willing to release individuals to use their gifts.

* **a good fit for the culture**

  Being at home in the context because they either come from the same/similar culture or are gifted in cross-cultural mission. Pay special attention to anyone who has sensed God's call to a particular group of people for some time.

3. Start with 'what they've got'

Successful founders of a fresh expression often start with what they've got - the priceless gifts that God has already given to them. These are represented in who they are, what they know and who they know.

If one or two people in your church are wondering whether they should start a fresh expression, you might ask them to talk about:

- **who they are;**

  Where do they live? Where do they work? What are their passions and interests?

- **what they know;**

  What are they good at? What expertise do they have?

- **who they know.**

  Who are their friends and networks? What are their family connections?

Then ask them, 'How might you use who you are and what you know to serve who you know?'

If someone is a sports coach working with teenagers, for example, might they coach one of the local teams, pair up with a Christian friend to provide good food after training, and see what the Spirit does in the conversations as they eat together?

One person hosted a sewing group in her home in sheltered accommodation. She said to herself, 'If I asked the assistant minister to visit us and say a pray at the end, could that be the start of something?'

In Poole, England, a common interest in felt making brought together two people, who started to run felt-making workshops. These sessions developed into a monthly felt-making group, which seeks to draw people into the Reconnect Christian community.

 Story: Reconnect - update Aug12
freshexpressions.org.uk/stories/reconnect/aug12

 web

In Paris, a woman and her husband stopped going to church, but still loved Jesus. They used what they'd got. The wife enjoyed welcoming guests ('who you are'), while her husband loved cooking ('what you know'). They invited four friends who were in limbo from church ('who you know'). Between them, they invited four others with little or no church background. They ate regularly together and discussed topics ranging from politics to personal lives to God. The wife told a conference that over the previous six to seven years, during which individuals had come and gone, four or five people had become Christians each year (*Being Church, Doing Life*, p46).

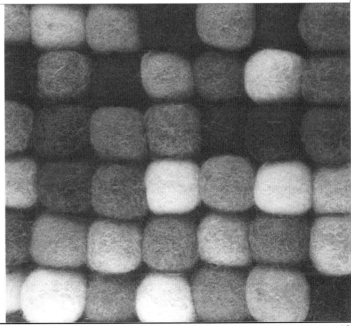

4. Allow time to gather a team

Just as it was not good for the man to be alone in Genesis 3, so it is not good for instigators of fresh expressions to pioneer on their own. They need to gather a team, however small. But this often takes time - and requires prayer and careful thought.

Pitfalls to avoid include:

- attracting disgruntled Christians, who are more preoccupied with what is wrong inside the church than with the missional opportunities outside it.

- gathering individuals who are unable to connect with the context - they live a long way from the housing estate or they are unable to identify with the people the initiative is called to serve.

- drawing in people who say they are available, but in practice are not. They are distracted by family, friendship or work commitments.

- gathering a team whose members have different spiritual bottom lines, don't get along well and can't agree on the vision.

- attracting individuals with pastoral problems, which become a distraction.

Explaining these pitfalls will help your fellow church leaders understand why the initiative may take longer than expected to come to fruition. They will be better able to encourage the founder - lay or ordained - in the difficult task of gathering a team. Patience is a priceless form of support.

Hot Chocolate

Story

Hot Chocolate was one of the first projects supported through the Emerging Ministries Fund in the Church of Scotland. As an independent youth work organisation, engaging with those aged 12-21, the Hot Chocolate Trust charity is based in the centre of Dundee, operating from The Steeple Church. Its aim is to continue to grow a Christian community *with* young people, not *for* young people - with them making the decisions about how, when and what happens, to draw in young people who are journeying to faith.

The Hot Chocolate team support the young people to develop a wide-ranging programme, including residentials, special interest groups and opportunities to explore their spirituality and contribute to their own fresh expression of church.

Charis Robertson, one of the leaders, says it had been an interesting context to have something growing up alongside the institutional church and - despite them setting out with no agendas and no predetermined plans - God had definitely been at work in the lives of the young people. The team have become more clear in their missional theology around belonging, believing and behaving and how the entry point for Hot Chocolate was around belonging. Hot Chocolate, though church-based, doesn't organise specific 'God slots' and the team instead see themselves as going on a journey with those involved.

Hot Chocolate immediately engages young people in the leadership of their own activities and plans and the responsibility for Hot Chocolate as a space belongs to them as a community. So building leadership within Hot Chocolate has become a very natural thing, with a deeply entrenched culture and expectation of that kind of responsibility and growth. In 2013, some of the young people started to describe Hot Chocolate as their church.

The long-term vision for Hot Chocolate and for the faith community is based around what a contextualised church looks like. For the people that have grown up through the organisation, questions will focus on 'What would it be like for them to lead the church? What would it be like for worship and prayer and liturgy to be written by them, liturgy that's completely relevant and owned by the community there?'

Effectuation: Elements of Entrepreneurial Expertise
Saras D Sarasvathy, Edward Elgar Publishing Ltd,
2009, 978-184844572-7

5. Encourage experimentation

Founders of fresh expressions usually improvise. They try one thing and then another. Often objectives become clarified and longer-term plans emerge only through this process of trial and error.

The story of Hot Chocolate (previous page), is a good example. The leaders did not start with a grand plan, they simply took cups of hot chocolate to young people in the centre of Dundee. The community has grown from there, step by step, in response to suggestions by and comments from the young people involved - and now has 6 paid staff working with 300 young people.

Experimentation involves trial and error. This means that some experiments won't work. It is vital to give founders of fresh expressions permission to fail. Failure is a way to learn. The team might ask, 'What have we learnt about what might work from our unsuccessful experiment?'

Saras Sarasvathy, who has researched successful entrepreneurs in the United States, has found that failing is an integral part of venturing well. Successful entrepreneurs are willing to fail. They outlive failures 'by keeping them small and killing them young' (*Effectuation*, p17).

We can think of fresh expression founders as 'ecclesial entrepreneurs', often working on a small scale. They see possibilities and start something. Failure is as important for them as for other types of entrepreneur, so keep giving them permission to fail. If they are hesitant about starting out, encourage them to try something small as a one off. Tell them, 'See what happens. Don't worry if it doesn't work. The point of an experiment is to learn something. Great advances have come from "failed" experiments - e.g. the discovery of penicillin. Even if it doesn't work, who knows what will come from it!' If your leaders or the congregation are holding back, encourage them to dip their toes in the water by trying one or two experiments. 'Let's try just one fresh expression and then prayerfully review the results.'

Put in proper support

Founders of fresh expressions should be helped and encouraged to access appropriate support.

What do I need?

Depending on the scale and type of initiative, those starting fresh expression of church will need:

- **someone to cry and laugh with;**
- **a spiritual director/companion;**
- **prayer support;**
- **training in the practice and theology of contextual church;**

  This should include the methodologies and skills needed at the particular stage of the venture. Might they attend a *mission shaped ministry* (*msm*) course? Better still, why don't the overseeing minister and founder attend together?

- **a coach or mentor;**

  They should not only listen, but advise, warn (without judging) and empower. Sometimes the team may need coaching or mentoring.

- **advice from someone who has started a church in a similar context or been involved in a comparable type of activity;**

  (e.g. working among disadvantaged young people).

- **peer support from other founders of fresh expressions;**
- **specialist expertise in finance, legal and other matters.**

This may seem a lot of support! But we live in an ever more sophisticated world, in which complex tasks are becoming more common for many people.

Don't underestimate the challenges involved in starting a new gathering, even a small one, and remember that the skills required may change from stage to stage: 'settling' a church may need different capabilities to 'birthing' it.

  mission shaped ministry
missionshapedministry.org

Oversight and accountability

Providing prayerful oversight and accountability is vital. You will find it helpful to have early conversations, including with your denominational leaders, around some of the questions below. Often answers will not yet be clear. In which case, agreeing when the question will be revisited, by whom and how, will help to avoid misunderstandings later.

Make it clear

Questions should include:

- how will the initiative be governed?

- how will leaders be appointed and for how long?

- what are the financial expectations and requirements (eg insurance)?

- how will appropriate safeguarding policies be implemented?

- how will the initiative be maintained if leaders of the sponsoring church/denomination change (often a problem)?

- how will progress be reviewed?

- how will the sacraments be celebrated (in cases where only ordained ministers can preside)?

For matters of policy and governance, it is helpful to have a simple constitutional document that clearly lays out the requirements and responsibilities.

Oversight can involve regular meetings with the minister or a wise lay person nominated by the minister or church council. It will be good practice:

- to agree with the founder what will be expected of him/her and what support will be available;
- to make sure that the supervisor and founder meet regularly and that they periodically evaluate the relationship;
- to expect the supervisor to champion the initiative and 'to smooth the way' in relation to the local church;
- to keep in mind throughout that the founder is accountable to the people the initiative serves, as well as to the sponsoring church (and to God, of course!);
- to be explicit about how often the founder will report to the church leadership and members and the form this will take. If the parent church is not kept updated, mistrust may arise, especially if things develop in unexpected ways;
- to separate accountability from support (which can be provided as suggested above). Though the founder should be held to account supportively, combining formal support and accountability risks one undermining the other.
- to keep accountability as light touch as possible. The supervisor should not second guess the founder, but should oversee and hold the person to account mainly through wise questioning (e.g. 'On what grounds do you think this?' 'How would you explain your decision to the rest of the church?').

Understand the mindsets involved

Accountability can become stressful if the parties involved don't understand and value the different mindsets they bring to the table.

The person offering supervision, who will often be a church leader, will frequently have an 'organisational' mindset. This mindset values:

- **goals:** 'we need to know what we are aiming to achieve';
- **plans:** 'we must set out how we are going to achieve our goals';
- **timelines:** 'who does what by when?';
- **written procedures:** 'everyone must know how we do things here';
- **job descriptions:** 'individuals must understand what is expected';
- **safe structures:** 'who's responsible for what?'.

These are entirely appropriate in an established organisation. They provide a stabilising skeleton and minimise unnecessary risks.

Founders of fresh expressions of church, however, often require a very different mindset. They are working in situations of uncertainty. When they start out, they don't know what will work and what won't, so they can't have clear goals.

They may be clear about wanting to work in a school context, for instance, but frequently they will be uncertain as to what form this will take. Possibly they have in mind a 'prayer space' or some form of Messy Church, but till they have listened further to families, teachers and others involved they cannot be sure they will travel in this direction.

If their goals are embryonic, they cannot have long-term plans with timelines to achieve them and all the rest. All they can do is to envisage a first step. So they will start not with a goal, but with the here-and-now, with what they've got - who they are, what they know and who they know.

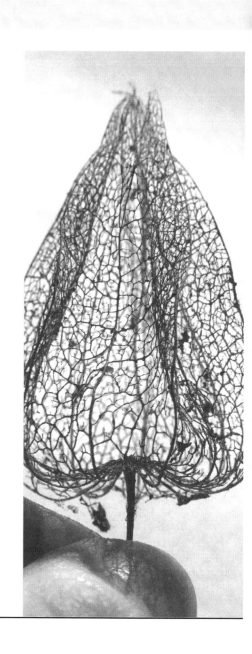

On this basis, they will get together with one or two other Christians and proceed step-by-step. 'Let's try this', the team may say, 'and see if it works'. They will improvise as they go along. They will seize opportunities. If one door closes, they will go through another - rather like St Paul in Acts 16.6-10. The route to Bithynia (in modern Turkey) was closed, so he and his colleagues went instead to Macedonia, which was in a totally different direction.

For those with an organisational mindset, supervising founders with a pioneering mindset can feel frustrating. 'So tell me what this fresh expression will look like', you ask. But instead of getting a concrete answer, you get some vague 'maybes' and 'coulds'. This doesn't mean that the other person cannot get it together, it reflects the appropriate uncertainty with which the founder is setting out.

Or perhaps the conversation goes like this:

> 'I thought six months ago we agreed that you were going to do something in the school, but now you are talking about the community centre.'

> 'Well, the centre's manager has changed and there is a golden opportunity. We can't miss it!'

> 'But you didn't tell me.'

> 'I'm telling you now!'

> 'It's not good enough. How can I possibly trust you if you don't do what you say?'

And so it continues till the relationship breaks down.

But this need not happen if both parties understand that they have different mindsets. The founder must realise that you need an organisational mindset if you are going to lead a church successfully. Indeed, founders themselves will require this mindset once their initiatives become firmly established. Goals, plans, timelines, procedures (however simple) and so on will become a necessary backbone of the new community.

Equally, those offering supervision must understand that 'we make it up as we go along' has become a mantra for most pioneers of fresh expressions. Founders need time and space to flow with the opportunities and see where the Spirit leads them.

One of the blessings of a blended or mixed-economy church is when organisational and pioneering mindsets rub shoulders together and learn from each other.

Supervision meetings

Make your supervision meetings fruitful and creative - they are an opportunity for mutual learning. Hopefully the founder will learn from your questions and wisdom, but equally, you can learn about fresh expressions from the founder's experience. You will then be better placed to champion the founder and encourage your church to embrace the new venture.

Pastoral cycle

Looking back and looking forward, in the context of prayer and perhaps Bible study, is an obvious way to structure your meetings. You might frame looking back round what is known as the pastoral cycle:

- **experience:** what has the founder experienced since you last met?

- **exploration:** what factors have shaped that experience? What's going on behind what's going on?

- **enquiry:** how does God see this, what would delight and disappoint him, what would Jesus do in the light of the journey so far?

- **enacting Jesus:** what should the founder do in the light of this exploration and enquiry, what next steps would reflect Jesus, how can the supervisor (or the sponsoring church) provide appropriate support?

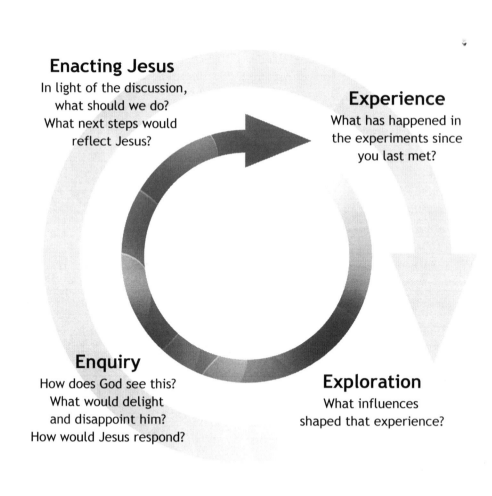

Enacting Jesus
In light of the discussion, what should we do? What next steps would reflect Jesus?

Experience
What has happened in the experiments since you last met?

Enquiry
How does God see this? What would delight and disappoint him? How would Jesus respond?

Exploration
What influences shaped that experience?

How can fresh expressions emerge? (Share booklet 01)
Michael Moynagh, Andy Freeman, Fresh Expressions, 2011, 978-095681231-5

What should we start? (Share booklet 03)
Michael Moynagh, Andy Freeman, Fresh Expressions, 2011, 978-095681233-9

freshexpressions.org.uk/share/booklets

Looking forward can go beyond the 'actions' that arise from looking back to ask questions about strategic direction. Questions built round 'a fresh expressions journey', described earlier, can encourage the founder to keep acting intentionally.

For example:

- **who else should the founder and team be listening to?**
- **how can the initiative love and serve the people it is called to reach?**
- **how might people experience community as the initiative develops?**
- **how can the team help individuals to explore discipleship?**
- **is the initiative developing in ways that will help it to be sustainable?**
  From the earliest days, for instance, what steps are being taken to indigenise leadership, so that leadership is shared with the new members of the community?
- **are paths being laid to discipleship, worship and Christian community?**
- **are emerging Christians being encouraged to start further fresh expressions of church in a segment of their lives?**

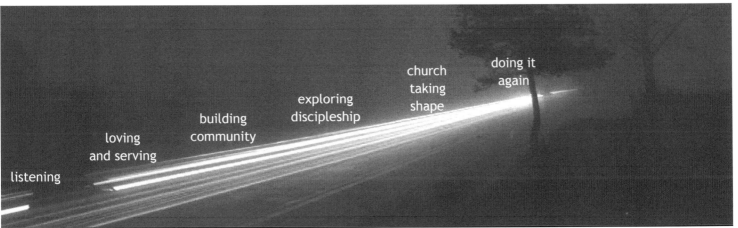

Discern fruitfulness

Though measurement and target-setting have had a bad press, Christians should not shy away from seeking to discern spiritual fruitfulness. In John 15, Jesus talks about the importance of being fruitful.

Giving an account

Accountability need not merely involve being accountable for achieving agreed targets. It can be understood more widely as giving an account of what you have been doing - describing what you have done, why you did it and what you now think about it.

Supporting a fresh expression should include asking, 'What are the signs that the Spirit is at work in the initiative? What can we learn from the presence and absence of these signs? Is the initiative getting some things right but not others? What does this mean for the next chapter of its life?'

Discerning fruitfulness may include quantifying, such as whether a growing number of people are being served by the project and how many are coming to faith. But it will go beyond this to also ask questions about the quality of the community's life, service and leadership.

One approach early on may be to ask questions based on 'a fresh expressions journey', described earlier (listening, loving and serving, building community, exploring discipleship, church taking shape, doing it again).

For example, what are the signs and evidence that:

- **the founding team is listening to the context effectively?**

  Might members record who has been listened to and list the main things they have learnt? Are there significant omissions? What has been the impact on their expectations and plans?

- **the initiative is fruitfully serving and loving the people it is called to?**

  How many people is it in touch with or serving regularly? Has the number grown? What are the benefits to those being reached? What is the feedback - and how is this being collected? What changes are planned as a result?

- **healthy community is emerging among those being served?**

  What steps have been taken to encourage community? How many people are involved in the main meeting and how often do they attend? Has the number grown? Is there evidence of community life between meetings (e.g. people meeting up informally) and what proportion of the group is involved in this? What is the feedback on people's experience of the community and what do you plan to do differently in the light of that?

- **people are beginning to explore becoming a disciple of Jesus?**

  Is there evidence of individuals having an interest in Jesus? What stepping stones have been laid to help individuals make journeys to Jesus? What has been the feedback? How many are being mentored one-to-one, have joined an explorers' group or have asked to be baptised? Has the number grown?

- **'church' is beginning to emerge?**

  Is there a regular act of worship and how many attend? What steps are being taken to deepen the experience of the Word and introduce the sacraments? What are the signs of new Christians wanting to grow in faith - how many attend Bible studies or are being discipled one-to-one for example? How are new Christians connecting to the wider church?

Being Church, Doing Life
Michael Moynagh, Monarch Books,
2014, 978-085721493-5

Book

These are only examples: you may want to ask questions that better fit your context.

You probably won't want to ask them all at once. If the initiative has travelled quite far along the fresh expressions journey, the founder and supervisor may want to review each bullet point in rotation over a year. They will need to interpret with care: fruit does not always appear quickly. Part of discernment is making a prayerful judgement about the appropriate length of gestation. You may be called to celebrate slow, small steps.

Once the initiative is well established, a different approach to evaluation may be appropriate. The book *Being Church, Doing Life* contains an appendix on how to evaluate fresh expressions of church.

One suggestion is that you ask questions based on the four interlocking sets of relationships that are central to church: with God (up), with the world (out), with the wider church (of) and within the fellowship (in). The appendix offers sample questions under each heading.

This type of approach will provide a structured way to hold the fresh expression to account and to report on its life to the parent church. As the latter gets used to receiving such a report, members might ask, 'Why don't we develop some equivalent questions about *our* activities?'

Web

GraceSpace

Story

The 'church for people who don't go to church' in Shipley, near Bradford, started life in 2007 through the setting up of Vicars Café in Saltaire, as part of a vision to create a community in the Aire Valley. The café eventually became a social enterprise.

The original community decreased in numbers but when pioneer minister Colin Blake was appointed for a five-year term, he soon discovered that eating together was vital to the making and sustaining of relationships.

People flocked to be part of it when GraceSpace came up with the idea of having a different meal theme for each Sunday in the month.

Colin had a clear mission focus for GraceSpace and recognised that it was very important to get strong building blocks of community in place right from the start. Looking to discipleship and sustainability also featured in those early plans which saw of a lot of events transferred from Vicars Café to Colin's own home.

Careful contextualisation was at the heart of GraceSpace's development as people began to meet together as a group around meals.

GraceSpace operates with a light touch. It doesn't have an 'official' structure, such as a PCC or Council, but people meet together every three months for a Summit meeting at which priorities are decided for the next quarter. Weekly 'Explore' sessions offer the chance to look at Bible application rather than Bible study.

Numbers have now grown and the GraceSpace community developed into a strong team when Colin suffered a period of illness. People offered their homes and skills to keep things moving along while he was out of action. He recognised that the illness prompted the devolving, training, encouraging and mentoring of others into leadership.

There are plans to create a second GraceSpace and members are considering how to look 'outside' and make a difference.

Relations with the wider church

If the founding team is to be a fresh expression in embryo, it must be connected to the wider church. Christians are baptised into, and find their identity in, the whole body of Christ. Wise support will encourage these links to be maintained.

Connection is key

Being connected may involve team members worshipping in their parent church on occasion (as well as worshipping together), belonging to a variety of Christian networks, and the team leader being in fellowship with the parent church's leadership and/or other Christian leaders in the area.

As individuals come to faith, it is important that they too forge ties to the wider church. This will make concrete their new identity in Christ and his body, help them to mature in the faith and encourage mutual blessing between new and older expressions of church.

Connecting up may range from taking part in Christian festivals and pilgrimages, to sharing events with their parent church, to accessing Christian books and online material.

As a first step, a fresh expression of church might offer to organise some games on a family fun day for the whole local church, or provide transport for those in the parent congregation wanting to attend a 'churches together' event, or serve coffee after a joint Easter celebration. There is nothing like serving to get involved with the wider church!

Supporting a fresh expression of church's founder includes discussing how the local church can deepen its relationship with the emerging Christian community.

The relationship must be two way. Just as wise parents allow their children to grow into adults who relate to them as equals, so the existing church must not use its size and influence to dominate its offspring. Rather, it should learn from the new insights that emerge in the fresh expression.

In denominations where only ordained ministers can preside, how holy communion is celebrated may need careful thought. If the fresh expression is led by a lay person, possibilities include:

- celebrating communion with the parent church from time to time;

- asking a minister from a church with whom the fresh expression has a relationship to preside, symbolising the gathering's connection to the wider church;

- holding an agape supper, in which the bread and wine are not consecrated, to remember Christ's death and resurrection in the context of eating together;

- making use of extended communion to allow the bread and wine to be consecrated in one gathering and distributed later in the other;

- in the Methodist Church, asking to have a lay person authorised to preside at communion: this is allowed in missional contexts, where otherwise it is agreed that communion would not be available.

VentureFX

Story

VentureFX is the Methodist Church's pioneering ministries scheme. By 2012 it had 14 pioneer ministers, who are part of a peer group learning and support network. Ian Bell, coordinator of VentureFX, personally visits each pioneer on a regular basis to address a range of concerns, both general and contextual.

As soon as a pioneer is appointed, arrangements are put in place for a local line management group to be set up. One of the group will become the pioneer's line manager - this could be a Circuit Superintendent or District Chair, but not necessarily so. The pioneer and line manager usually meet monthly to focus on practicalities of the project and the individual's personal development; the management group as a whole meets the pioneer about once a quarter.

Be warned! Putting in proper support can lead to confusion as to supervisory responsibility and the lines of accountability. Ian does not look to duplicate or conflict with the oversight of the local line management but instead aims to offer a wider perspective, looking at how a local situation is affecting the individual's calling to be a pioneer and what learning and good practice might be worth sharing with others across the VentureFX scheme.

An oversight session between Ian and a pioneer is nearly always over a meal, where discussion ranges from what has happened since they last met, to reflecting on the good and bad along the way. It is not about telling the pioneer what they should or should not have done, but much more along the lines of a mentor role, talking about the challenges ahead and 'joining the dots' for them. The idea is to properly supervise, not 'over-control'. It is important to help the pioneers explore new opportunities that may have come up in their contexts by teasing out the implications of that opportunity and seeing if it would help them to achieve what they are looking to do as part of the bigger picture.

Being part of a peer network meeting monthly also means that the pioneers watch over one another in love. It's a mistake to assume that because pioneers are creative they don't need affirmation in what they do. At times, hard questions have to be asked by those overseeing what's happening, but if a strong relationship has been built up with the pioneer in question, those hard questions will not be detrimental to that relationship or destroy it.

Pastoral ministry and innovation

Whether you are a pastor or an innovator, you still have a role in catalysing and supporting fresh expressions in your local church.

Conclusion

Some ministers are reluctant to get involved with fresh expressions because they think it is not their calling: they are called to the pastoral ministry. Yet good pastoring is exactly what founders need!

Ministers overseeing a fresh expressions have a particular responsibility to interpret the initiative to the existing congregation and wider church, to help clear a pathway for the founder and to ensure that the founder is held to account and properly supported. To do this, you require good pastoral gifts.

So if you feel called to pastoral ministry, you could be just the person to encourage fresh expressions of Christian community in your local church. You don't need to be doing the pioneering yourself - others in the congregation can take the initiative. What those who start a fresh expression of church need more than anything is good pastoral support.

With your pastoral gifts you can be:

- an encourager;
- a sounding board;
- a source of probing questions;
- a warning voice;
- an interpreter of what the person is doing, especially to others who do not understand.

Of course, if you see yourself as an innovator, you can bring those gifts to bear.

2nd edition
Published 2014 by Fresh Expressions
Registered charity #1080103

Copyright © Fresh Expressions 2014
freshexpressions.org.uk

Fresh Expressions, CDO, 1 Hill Top,
Coventry, CV1 5AB
0300 365 0563

Author: Michael Moynagh
Series Editor: Karen Carter
Series Designer: Ben Clymo

freshexpressions.org.uk/share/booklets

ISBN 978-0-9575684-1-9

Related resources

expressions: making a difference
(Fresh Expressions, 2011)

 A DVD containing 28 stories illustrating the lessons to be learnt as fresh expressions of church make a difference to people's lives.

Available from
freshexpressions.org.uk/shop

freshexpressions.org.uk/guide

 The Guide contains how-to-do-it advice on starting, developing and sustaining fresh expressions of church.

freshexpressions.org.uk

 Further stories and information, plus audio and video material and resources to download and purchase.

1st edition published 2012
ISBN 978-0-9568123-9-1